The Bigly Beautiful Book
of
What Women Want

by D. J. Drumpf

Illustrated by N. O. Fawkes

First printing 2017

ISBN-13: 978-0692843482

ISBN-10: 0692843485

This book is dedicated to the nasty women of the world. You know who you are, and you know what you really want.

Women want . . .

AFFECTION

Kiss them before you say hello.

Grab 'em by the privates, if you're famous.

(Remember to use Tic-Tacs first.

Bad breath is disgusting.)

Women want . . .

A MAN WHO LOVES CHILDREN

Talk about dating your daughter.
(Be sure to mention that sex
is what you have in common.)

Women want . . .

INTIMACY

Hover over them in voting booths.

(And sneak up behind them at televised

debates.)

Women want . . .

A GUY WHO LOVES ANIMALS

Clever pet names,
like "pig" and "dog," will let them know
exactly what kind of guy you are.
(Ranking their appearance on a scale
from 1 to 10 also shows you've been
thinking about them.)

Women want . . .

TO BE SPOILED

I like to leave cash on the nightstand.

(Russian girls now take Bitcoin.)

Women want . . .

SURPRISES

I like to surprise them
when they're changing clothes.
(Especially at beauty pageants.)

Women want . . .

UNDERSTANDING

Understand that if a woman asks you a
difficult question, it's probably because
there's blood
coming out of her wherever.
(By which, of course, I meant her ears.)

Women want . . .

A HAND TO HOLD

My hands

are about the same size as a woman's.

(ALT FACT: Women are known to have

YUGE hands.)

Women want . . .

TO KNOW WHO'S IN CHARGE

So remember to treat her like shit.
(To keep her from becoming a nasty
woman.)

Women want . . .

FREEDOM

That's why, when it comes to wives,

I practice catch-and-release.

(Now serving #3.)

Women want . . .

MYSTERY

So lie constantly.

(And never let her see your tax returns.)

Women want . . .

SECURITY

I'm okay with that.

(If I don't keep them locked up,

they tend to escape.)

Women want . . .

TO LAUGH

I just wish they didn't do that so much
when I'm naked.
(It hurts my feelings.)

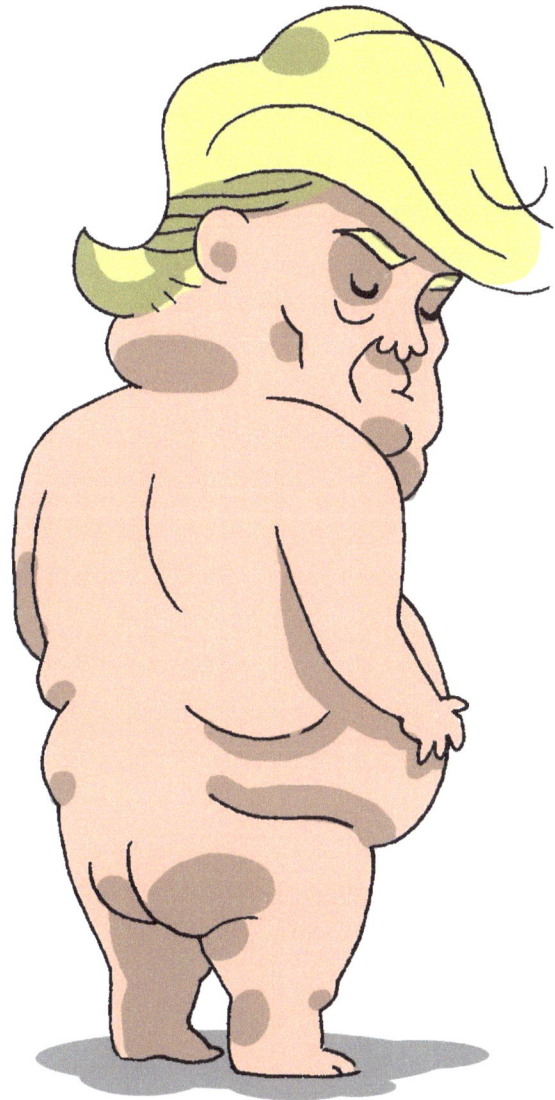

Women want . . .

TO FEEL APPRECIATED

If I come home and dinner's not ready,

I go through the roof.

(It lets them know you care.)

Women want . . .

EQUAL PAY FOR EQUAL WORK

Which seems totally unfair.

(Sad.)

Women want . . .

A MAN WITH A
GENEROUS HEART

I spread my love around.

(My wives almost seem relieved.)

www.ingramcontent.com/pod-product-compliance
Lightning Source LLC
Chambersburg PA
CBHW042103040426

42448CB00002B/122